RONNIE BARKER'S

Book of Boudoir Beauties

HODDER & STOUGHTON
London Sydney Auckland Toronto

"There is a destiny that shapes our ends" *William Shakespeare*
"The definition of a good girl is one who only undresses once every twenty-four hours" *Oliver Cromwell*
"Two's company" *British Brassiere Co.*

BIBLIOGRAPHY

The History of the Bed . . . . Arthur Negus

The History of Beds . . . . Bedfordshire County Council

Tits as Companions . . . . Welsh Cage-bird Society

CONTENTS

Introduction

In the companion volume to this work, entitled Ronnie Barker's Book of Bathing Beauties, I offered a treatise on the wonders and eccentricities of the female form, as depicted on Picture Postcards.

This book is also devoted to the same end (or ends—see page 83) but we are concerned, for the most part (or parts—see page 83) with what goes on behind closed doors, and shuttered windows, as opposed to what goes on or comes off in the free-for-all atmosphere of the beach.

A very different kettle of fish, you will say; those of you who are in the habit of keeping fish in kettles, that is. How does this chap, a mere strolling player, who struts on the stage and does fret-work; how does *he* know what goes on behind shut lockers and closed drawers? What makes him *au fait* with the *Boudoir*, apart from a slight smattering of French?

I can only suggest that you A read the book or B take my word for it that I am a man of some experience where Boudoirs are concerned, having actually BEEN IN THREE OF THEM.

I have been greatly assisted in the parts of this work which deal with Etiquette and Social Behaviour, by a member of the aristocracy (Gladys, Duchess of Bloemfontein, who served in Paris during the First World War, and who now drinks in my local). In all other particulars I have relied upon my own judgement, based upon the three boudoirs mentioned above, some theatrical digs in Llandudno, and a fortnight spent working in a pork butchers.

But let us waste no more time on excuses. The pictures themselves are, I hope, enough reason for the book's existence: and the various appendices, appendages, addenda, memorabilia and errata throughout should provide handy hints for the man in the street, while at the same time producing snorts of derision from the experts.

Let us then approach the boudoir door, grasp the handle firmly, and peep inside. . . .

(N.B. There is a special appendix on First Aid in the Bedroom; this is intended for the layman only—in the case of Doctors or Surgeons, the appendix should be removed at once)

R.B.

A Preliminary Note

WHAT IS A BOUDOIR?

Before we go any further, let us get one thing clear. Everybody does it. Rich or poor, old or young. The lady who serves you with your groceries does it. So does the policeman on the beat. Royalty certainly do it, as often as anyone else. Big businessmen do it; and so do little businessmen—(only in a much smaller way, naturally). I have heard that some millionaires have it done for them; but most of us prefer to do it ourselves. I refer, of course, to undressing; and the inevitable eventual consequence of such an action— dressing again. The girls in the following pages illustrate the many and varied types of dresser and undresser to be encountered in the boudoir to which this slim volume, and fat author, are devoted.

SECTION ONE· DRESSING AND UNDRESSING

Snappy Dressers

A beautiful example of the girl who dresses to please. Crisp white chemise, dainty pink bows above the knee, and the hat, giving that extra touch where it's most needed. And with good strong elastic to hold everything up, a truly snappy dresser, who can be heard undressing three rooms away.

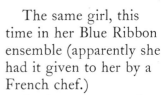

The same girl, this time in her Blue Ribbon ensemble (apparently she had it given to her by a French chef.)

Again a pretty outfit, but rather more complicated. The first time she wore it, she tied several of the ribbons incorrectly; later, in Regent Street, she raised her arm to hail a cab, and threw herself flat on her back.

Sloppy, Slipshod & Slapdash Dressers

Many girls, I fear, fall into this category. Simply leaping out of bed, throwing on the first thing that comes to hand, gulping down a cup of coffee and leaving for the office.

This girl actually got as far as Sloane Square Underground station before realizing her mistake. She tried to cover herself with her umbrella, only to find it was a walking stick. However, she quickly stuck the hatbox over her head, and finished the journey safe in the knowledge that she couldn't be recognized.

Thin legs are, and have always been, a distinct disadvantage where stockings are concerned. The elastic just won't bite.

What is the answer? Fatter legs (see page 66).

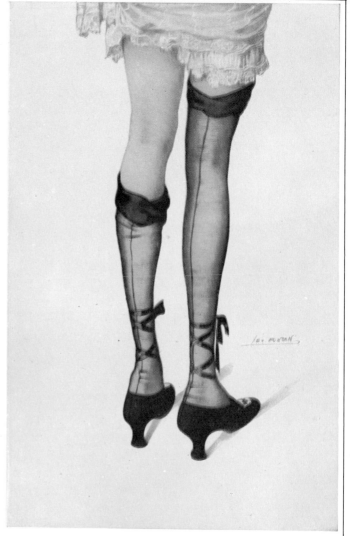

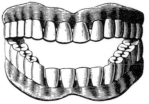

The "dreamer" (or "mooner" as she would be known in Bedfordshire) is the most unsatisfactory dresser of all. She dreams (or moons) her way round the Boudoir grabbing bundles of underwear and draping it here and there on her person, her mind on other things. . . .

"I wonder who'll be at the dance tonight. . . . I wonder if someone will bring me home. . . . I wonder what that thing is round my leg . . ."

... Maybe I shouldn't have
had sherry
at lunchtime ... I wonder
where my mauve
jacket is....

". . . Oh, there's me jacket. It was on me arm
all the time. Right, almost ready then. Oh,
gawd, I haven't got me vest on. Mum! Tell
Nobby to keep his hair on, I'll be another
twenty minutes."

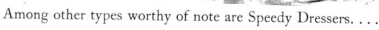

Among other types worthy of note are Speedy Dressers. . . .

La coquetterie
Coquetry

. . . Slaphappy Dressers. . . .

. . . and of course, Welsh
Dressers. This is a fine
example of a late 19th-
Century Welsh Dresser
(kindly loaned by Arthur
Negus).

Top Dressing

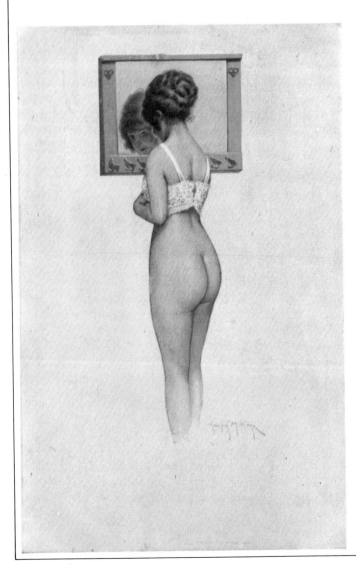

A favourite method; depending, of course, on different girls' points of view.

Top Dressing is much in favour by gardeners. My own gardener, however, is of the opinion that they are like onions—when you've seen two, you've seen them all.

What to Wear

So far so good

At the risk of sounding negative, I feel perhaps this section should be called "what *not* to wear", as the Boudoir is notorious for turning out some extraordinary get-ups (as the following pages show).

This girl, for instance, who is about to drop her bloomers (onto a chair) appears to be wearing her husband's socks.

Safety First Note
(see illustration below)
Never, under any circumstances, hang your knickers over the oil lamp.

Another mistake. This girl is sporting on her head what is without question a chamber pot and flue-brush.

Here, a rather more sensible approach. A complete woollen bodystocking. Ideal for the Boudoir, giving warmth, freedom of movement, and the feeling of relaxation that only nudity can bring; but with the comforting thought that should the insurance man suddenly turn up, she would be comprehensively covered.

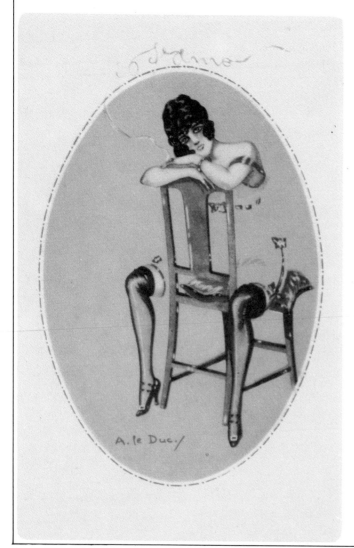

A. le Duc./

Underwear to match your Boudoir colour-scheme is very popular, but can be carried to extremes — witness this macabre effect (known as the "disappearing chemise").

A Word about Hats

Hats—with very few exceptions (see page 7) are seen to their best advantage when worn on the head. This goes without saying, like a dumb-waiter.

However, hats in the Boudoir are not to be encouraged. The answer to the question "Why not?" is to be found overleaf.

(Note: one disadvantage is illustrated here. This girl is so occupied with her hat that she has failed to notice that her knickers have fallen down.)

PRIX-FIXE

The answer, of course, is Woman's crowning glory, the hair (or hairs, as they are known medically). Here we see some of those crowning glories . . . "cascading in luxuriant waves around her shoulders, reaching almost down to that beautiful pair of magnificent chrysanthemums, which nestle quietly in a fold in the Surrey hills" (R.A.C. Handbook, 1912).

Indeed, the Boudoir is just the place for a woman to let her hair down. . . .

... but of course, there are limits.

And if you *must* wear a hat, don't be embarrassed about it. Wear it with pride, as a standard-bearer carries his flag. (But not in the same place, of course).

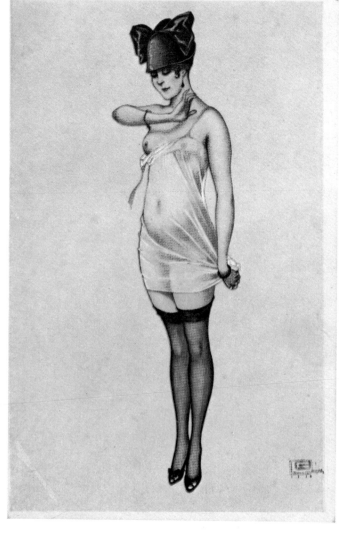

SECTION TWO·BEHAVIOUR IN THE BOUDOIR

"YES DEAR, I'VE NOTICED HOW TIMID OUR NEW·CURATE IS. IN FACT AT CHRISTENINGS HE'S SO NERVOUS HE ALWAYS WETS HIMSELF AS WELL AS THE BABY."

With Visitors

This section is self-explanatory—a few illustrated tips on how to treat a visitor (also when, and, in some cases, with what).

With a female visitor there is usually very little difficulty. Simply take tea, and engage in conversation similar to the above.

It is with the male visitor however, that the following pages are most concerned.

Naturally, if his attentions are unwelcome, a girl must not (a) let him take his coat off; (b) let him take her dress off; (c) let him put the light off. *But* if, on the contrary, she welcomes his advances, then see over. . . .

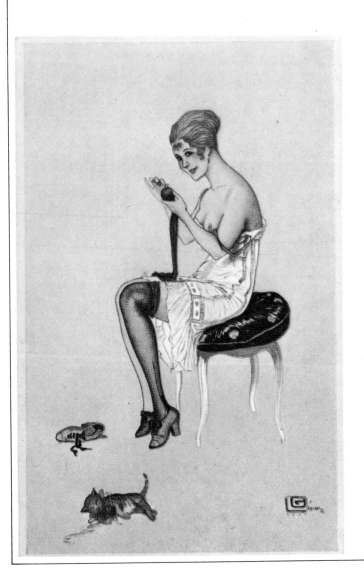

For a start, the worst thing a girl can do is to carry out domestic chores during his visit. No young executive, anxious to get to the top of the ladder, will want to sit there watching her mend it.

A girl should never try
to be too nonchalant
(never lie on the floor
just to show off your new
shoes) . . .

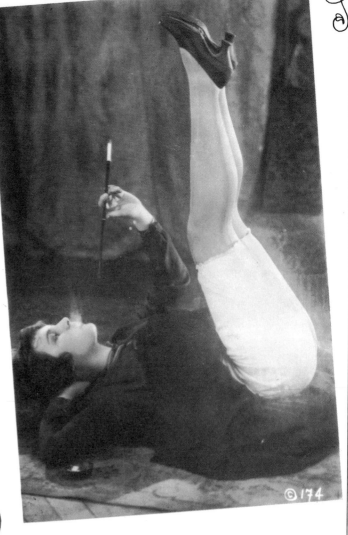

8573

HONEY, DOES YER LOVE ME?

W. T. W. 29. 1. 1905

... Or go out of her way to appear comic.

If you appear too forward he may lose respect for you (this applies especially to older women; one wrong move, and he'll be down those stairs, and off).

On the other hand, being ready to defend one's honour to this extent will probably frighten him off anyhow. (This is actually a photograph of a well-known landlady in Colwyn Bay, whose motto was "Stand by to repel all boarders".)

Dressing up can be fun. Try dressing as a maid and waiting by the front door, ready to respond to a tap on the knocker.

But beware, lest he prove unfaithful and make a pass at you, thinking you are the maid, while he thinks you are out of the room.

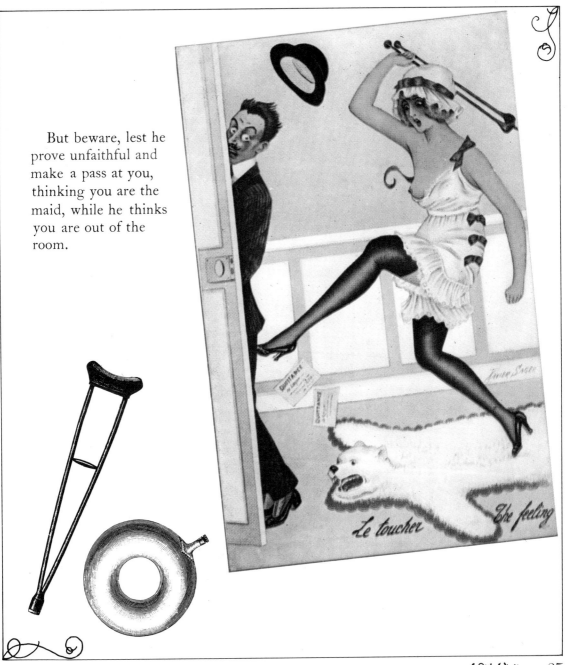

Pretending you had forgotten he was coming, and shouting "Come in, Mildred" at the sound of his knock can prove effective in dealing with the more bashful suitor.

But make sure it isn't the gas-man's day to call — otherwise he may spend twenty minutes checking your boiler.

Far better to welcome him in an informal and cosy atmosphere. This girl believes in having something warm and furry to welcome her gentleman caller, and put him at his ease.

Finally, above all, be
yourself—let your own
personality shine through. As the
poet T. W. Hughes so aptly
wrote:-

Silks and laces, airs and graces
All are right, in different places
But beneath it all—agree it—
You're a girl! So let him see it.

Below: Design for an Xmas decoration.
(*The Haberdashers Weekly*, 1898)

What needs to be said? This is the very function for which a boudoir came into being.

The definition of Boudoir (according to the *Popular Encyclopaedia*, or *Conversations Lexicon*, published by Blackie and Son about 1890) is "a small room, simply and gracefully fitted up, destined for retirement — from the French '*bouder*' — to pout, to be sulky".

In other words, a place where you can bathe your aching feet. . . .

. . . boil the kettle for a
nice cup of tea . . .

. . . or even try a thimbleful of the hard stuff. Which
brings us naturally to . . .

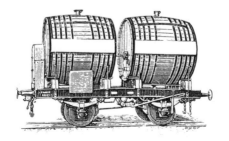

Breakfast in Bed

ere again, a great deal depends on whether one is breakfasting alone, or with a guest.

Alone, a girl can do as she pleases, even to the extent of perching on the bedside table for her early-morning gasper.

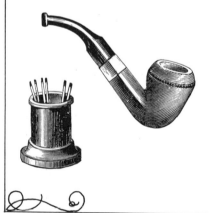

However, in the case of a shared breakfast, this sort of behaviour is much more acceptable.

Why not offer him a little fruit? Or, if he prefers it, let him help himself.

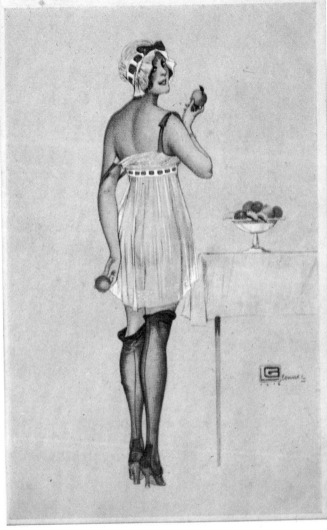

This approach (hiding cherries in the underclothing) while appearing at first sight to be fun, can result only in a lot of squashed cherries and breakfast eventually being abandoned altogether.

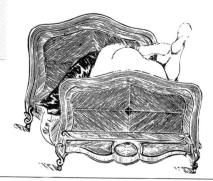

La gourmandise
Greediness

Above all, don't sit there making a pig of yourself.

Games & Pastimes

A few illustrations are here included, merely as suggestions.

1. GLASS BLOWING
(good lungs needed)

2. FLEA TRAINING
(good eyesight needed)

3. BOWLING
(an example of Women's Lob)

4. SKIPPING.

This is *either* a photograph of the Duchess of Bloemfontein when a girl (see introduction) *or* her brother Algy, dressed as Marie Lloyd. The Duchess herself isn't sure. "He and I were just like two little peaches on a tree. Especially him."

5. And then, of course, there's always darts. "A bulls-eye with the men," says the Duchess, who is not without experience in this area, having (in her youth) been voted "Miss double-top" by the United Dairies social club, and "Miss Two Nineteens" by the "Tailor and Cutter" (1921).

SECTION THREE: ENTERTAINING IN THE BOUDOIR

Drinks

ne of the most popular ways of entertaining in the Boudoir is, without doubt, inviting people to pop in for drinks.

This delightful girl seen wrestling with a wayward cork says champagne is one of the ways in which she retains the interest of her gentlemen callers. "I keep plunging it into cold water," she says. "This means I've always got something nice and cool to offer him in the evening."

Or how about a nice barrel of beer in the corner?

Of course, drink has other uses: for instance, disposing of the unwanted guest, by getting him plastered.

In any event, make
sure *you* don't over-indulge,
otherwise you yourself
may fall asleep; and if
there are several guests
present, who knows what
might go on in your
absence.

4 - Griserie

If in doubt, stick to coffee. At least you will know you are still on your feet.

"COFFEE FOR TWO."

Cooking in the Bedroom

FIG. 275. Showing cuts of beef in the live animal.

1. Head; 2. neck; 3. shoulder (chuck); 4. forerib; 5. middle rib; 6. loin; 7. rump; 8. hip; 9. brisket; 10. shouldered clod; 11. plate and navel; 12. flank; 13. round; 14. mouse buttock; 15 and 16. second cut round; 17. shank.
First quality: 4, 6, 7, 8, 14, and tongue; second quality: 5, 10, 13, 15, 16; third quality: 3, 12; fourth quality: 1, 2, 9, 17.

Here is a diagram of the various cuts of beef, showing what every good cook should know about a young bull. (*To be continued*)

N.B. A special "DON'T"
(*see right*)

And conversely, what every young
bull should know about a good cook.
(For key see previous page)

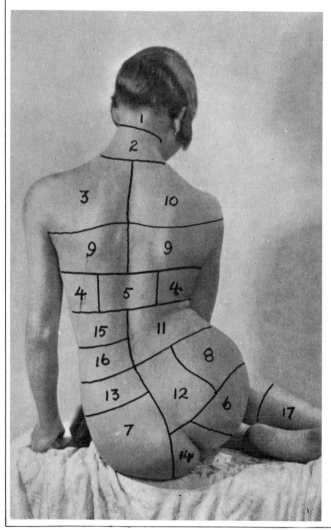

Entertaining the Troops

Our gallant French allies of World War One were noted for their sorties into the Boudoir. Some were experienced in battle, others were not.

This lad, for instance, certainly gives the impression that he has yet to go over the top.

"Aur innocents les mains pleines"

*Tout près de vous, mon âme énivrée de bonheur
Aspire à d'autres joies que lui dicte le cœur.*

Paris, overcrowded and full of troops, meant a hectic and disorganized life for the Parisian girl (often two of them sharing a bed-sitter, both entertaining at the same time). This led inevitably to tossing-up for whose turn it was on the chaise longue; frequently having to dine on occasional tables . . .

Du Front
à Table

Tu m'affoles !!!

DIX
PARIS
1159/5

. . . and occasionally having occasions on dining
tables.

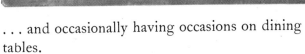

42 BAL BULLIER

Vive les Étudiants
Qui ont des femmes et pas d'enfants

Maurice

Parisiens Students
Knows how to have good times

Parties at the Flat

On the subject of parties, the Duchess of Bloemfontein is adamant. "If you are having a do and you don't know the do's and don't's, don't have a do." However, she freely admits that she herself had many a do before she knew what and what not to do. "And I'll have a few more before I'm done".

The above illustration is an artist's impression of the New Year's Eve party given at her Cadogan Square flat some years ago.

However, as she points out "The rascally butler put something into the punch—something of his own, you know. Out of spite."

The result can be seen on the following page.

This is another artist's on-the-spot impression of the same party four hours later. This second impression is much more accurate and detailed than the first, because, as the artist himself said, "I had a much easier task, as nobody moved for two days. Anyway,   it's a photograph".

On being shown the picture the Duchess remarked, "That's the trouble with this sort of Fancy Dress Party. A lot of masked balls finish up naked".

Here we see the Duchess herself, at her first fancy dress party. "This was also my first encounter with a member, if you will pardon the word, of the opposite sex."

In her own memoirs *"The Weight of the Aristocracy"* (Hodder $12\frac{1}{2}$p) she recalls vividly how much the young man admired her skirt.

All went swimmingly, apparently, until he tried to persuade her to put her cards on the table. "I wouldn't have minded," she said, "but it was the billiard table".

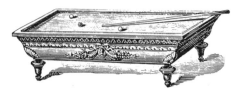

One should always be on one's guard against gate crashers and interlopers.

This ladies' orchestra (seen above) which was booked to play at a soirée for female nudists in Berkshire, recently, is here the subject of a simple quiz for the would-be party-giver.

Question: What is different about the girl with the arrow? (answer on the next page).

Clue: See illustration (right).

Yes, you've guessed it—they were all men, except for Linda (left). A second glance at the previous photograph may make many people wonder how they ever got past the front door in the first place. The fact remains that because the guests expected to see a ladies' orchestra, they *saw* a ladies' orchestra. It was only much later, when the orchestra found out that they too were required to undress, that things began to look different.

(Note: for a solution to the *Clue* on the previous page, please write to the publishers.)

Physical Charades—a must for any Boudoir party. Clothing should be loose and flowing, a nice big space cleared on the carpet—and onlookers should stand on tables, looking down, to obtain the best effect. A few simple "props" are needed to help the illusion, but these can usually be found lying around the average flat or house; in this case a circular silver tray, a length of something on fire at one end, and a set of false teeth three feet long.

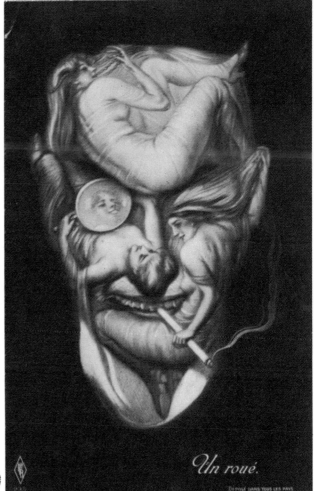

Un roué.

Bedroom Staff

This should be kept to a minimum. In these modern times, a good secretary is often worth employing, especially if one is entertaining business-men, who may suddenly feel the need for dictation.

Filmart ©

C126

One lady's maid should be kept, but beware of employing the pert city girl. She will never be off the phone, making local calls, sprawled all over the furniture, distracting your callers, and getting them to look up her numbers.

"WHAT 'DARNED' WORK THIS IS!"

Far better to employ a nice, homely country girl, who can be relied upon to be discreet and darn your visitors' socks at the same time.

Useful Extras

FOR YOUR BOUDOIR

For music lovers, almost essential for any boudoir—a gramophone, and a supply of records.

A safety note: remember always to shut the lid. Otherwise it is possible to sit back on it accidentally while it is in motion—a disastrous move, resulting in (a) the sitter being flung across the room, or (b) nasty scratches which may ruin the quality of the performance and, in extreme cases, prevent further reproduction altogether.

A handy false leg, for photographers. This is a boon when being photographed. It simply stands (on a stand) behind the body of the lady. Not only does it remain rigid and still for the photographer; it also prevents an enormous amount of strain on the part of the model.

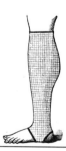

Here it is again—a different model, but the same old leg.

A few "Don'ts"

DON'T adjust your clothing when visitors are present.

DON'T appear in
crumpled underwear
(otherwise your guest may
feel he comes second in
your affections).

DON'T be shy. If you turn your back, it looks rude. He may go off in a huff (or even a hearse).

SECTION FOUR · FIT FOR ANYTHING

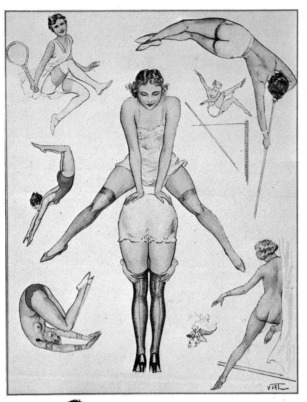

"A healthy boudoir is a happy boudoir" (*Die letztenyungfrau Geblitz,* 1909).

This quotation, obscure though it certainly is, sums up the few pages which follow: the magnificent specimen seen here (in her track suit) measures a stupendous 42-44-46.

Any girl who wishes to lead a full social life *must* look after her health. She must be able to go to sleep late, rise early, get dressed quickly, dance divinely, skip ecstatically, run like a gazelle, spring like a tiger . . .

. . . and generally bend over backwards to please people.

Housework, instead of being a drudge, can be made use of in the fight to be fit.

This girl (right) had been married for six months, and every night, when her husband came home, she was bent over the wash-tub: and she soon got very tired of it. Now, since she has continued the chore with a bending and stretching exercise, she once more enjoys it—and her smalls get done in half the time.

Below: An exercise which can be very useful should the man call to read the gasmeter.

Left-hand gasmeter   Right- hand gasmeter

Another grand way of exercising is simply
to be an animal in your Boudoir . . .

Why not be a Camel?

Or a Horse . . .

Or an Elephant . . .

. . . or even an ostrich. ("But don't try this
in sand," says Gladys*, "it gets
everywhere".)

* Duchess of Bloemfontein (see page 62) who served in Egypt twice.

Sitting, Standing, and Lying Down

An important part of any girl's behaviour in front of visitors. Nothing looks more ridiculous than someone sitting or standing awkwardly, as the above examples show.

And this, I'm afraid, can only be described as sprawling.

How to lie down. Place the body in a recumbent position (horizontal) with the face upwards and the back downwards. Relax most of the muscles, and assume a serene yet proud expression.

N.B. The body can also be positioned with the face downwards and the back upwards, according to individual taste.

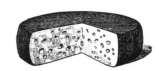

Interlude: A Cautionary Tale

She:
I know—you've come
about the rent.
I fear I don't possess
a cent;
And you—you look
so affluent!
(This fur is most
magnificent)
   (*continued*)

I really am most
penitent
And if it please you,
I'm content
Humbly to take my
punishment.
(Pray, tell me,
do you like my scent?)
                    (*continued*)

That eyeglass makes you
  look a gent.
My sight is bad;
  three pounds I spent
On glasses, but the frames
  got bent
(I really don't know
  where they went)
    (*continued*)

It seems that I cannot
prevent
The advent of this
sweet event
Come, sir, you have
my full consent
(You'll find me not
indifferent)
(*continued*)

She:
Well, Toby dear, he came
and went—
I've saved my cash for
nourishment.
His visit here was
Heaven-sent—
I'm now a paid-up
resident!

Toby
Miss Pearl,
don't think me impudent
I fear there's been an
accident:
Your eyesight's most
incompetent—
HE's not the man who takes
the rent!

THE END

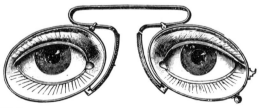

Appendix: First Aid in the Bedroom

Why should one ever need such a service? I hear you ask. The answer is contained in this stupid picture. As long as people continue to behave in a careless and irresponsible manner, the bandages and splints must never be far away.

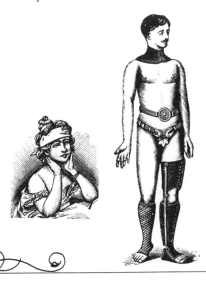

It comes high, but I must have it.

Here, too, we have an ever-present danger — the risk of fire. This love-sick girl with the candle could easily ruin the chances of a successful love-affair by holding it in such a careless and slip-shod manner: and even the man's candle is hardly at the correct angle.

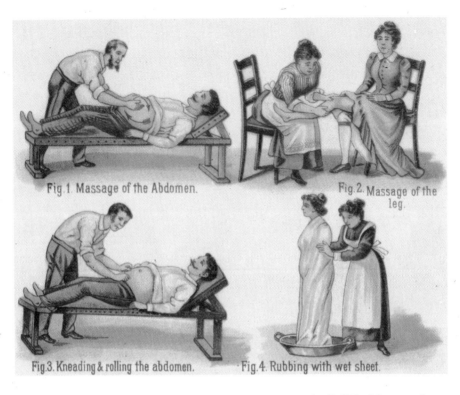

Fig.1. Massage of the Abdomen.

Fig.2. Massage of the leg.

Fig.3. Kneading & rolling the abdomen.

Fig.4. Rubbing with wet sheet.

An illustration from "*What to do on a rainy day*" (Hodder 15p).

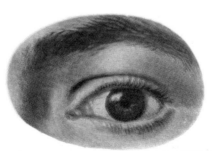

An example of
Butler's Disease
(Keyhole
conjunctivitis)

FIG. 16.—Portable hot air bath.

FIG. 60.—Application of tourniquet.

2 Breast Exhauster in use

FIG. 230. Hot-air bath for the shoulder.

A few useful illustrations from the *Knife-Grinders
Gazette* and other publications. (This should be pinned
to the ceiling for instant reference.)